Letters To My Sisters in Christ

Biblical devotional readings designed
to encourage Christians in their
daily walk with Christ.

CHRIS TRAINOR

WESTBOW
PRESS®
A DIVISION OF THOMAS NELSON
& ZONDERVAN

WestBow Press books may be ordered through booksellers or by contacting:

WestBow Press
A Division of Thomas Nelson & Zondervan
1663 Liberty Drive
Bloomington, IN 47403
www.westbowpress.com
844-714-3454

ISBN: 978-1-6642-8853-9 (sc)
ISBN: 978-1-6642-8852-2 (e)

Print information available on the last page.

WestBow Press rev. date: 02/24/2023

Dedication

To my 3 biological sisters who walked and still walk the journey of my life with me. They have inspired me, helped me, laughed and cried with me. I am forever grateful, Lu, Nan, and Mary. I also would like to thank my daughter, Denise, friends and family for encouragement along the way.

With love,
Chrissie

Foreword

Many years ago (about 36), I volunteered to write the monthy newsletter for a local chapter of Women's Aglow, a women's praise and prayer group. As I was thinking and planning on how to go about this, the Lord led me to think about including a short devotion each month. I've always considered myself someone like Moses who did not believe he had a "vocal" voice to share what was in his heart, but the Lord encouraged me, pointing out that it was not "vocal," but a written voice required for this endeavor. With the leading of the Lord, the inspiration of the Holy Spirit and my electric typewriter, I began to write down what I was taught as I studied and listened to God's voice and Word. These devotions are the result, crafted as Letters to my Sisters in Christ.

When I read these words from long ago (with some new ones along the way), I wondered about their relevance today. Then God reminds me that His Word is always alive, active and sharper than any two edged sword; always in the present to give us redemptive power over sin, and not subject to chronological space or time. So, I send you these letters with the love of Christ, praying that they will be "breathed anew," and will do their perfect work in our hearts and lives. I am eternally grateful for you, my sisters in Christ. May our Father, through Jesus Christ, richly bless you.

Sincerely, Chris Trainor

PS: I have included a few passages from various places. Most are " anonymous," but if I know the source, I have included it.

PART I

BEAUTIFUL TRUTHS REVEALED TO ORDINARY PEOPLE WALKING AN INTIMATE JOURNEY WITH JESUS

August, 1986

Dear Sisters in Christ,

Faith. The gift of God. It soars above the realm of the five senses as an eagle soars above a deep canyon, the depth of which does not affect its flight. So often walking by faith is confused with feelings. In truth, faith is of the spirit, feelings are of the flesh. Jesus says in John 6:63 [KJV] that in a spiritual sense, "The flesh profits nothing." Our feelings change continually, but God's truth is constant. Faith simply allows God's words to prevail over sense evidence. Webster defines "prevail" as "To be or become effective," also, "To triumph." When we make the decision to believe what God says about our circumstances and decisions, instead of sense evidence or the exercise of reason, we make God's Word and Will to become effective in our experience. For example, the Shunamite woman of 2 Kings 2:26 [AMP] confessed to the prophet's servant, "It is well," despite the fact that her son lay dead in the house. Her faith was speaking to the effecting of the miracle of his resurrection by God through the prophet. It wasn't reasonable for her to say, "It is well," but faith takes what reason can't.

I encourage myself and you also, to get beyond the flesh and to agree with God, not allowing a lack of "feeling fervent" to keep us from His presence. Let's go boldly unto His throne of grace, leaving flesh and reason outside the door, to worship Him in Spirit and Truth!

Bless the Lord,
From Chris

June, 1993

Dear Sisters in Christ,

This month I'd like to share a few thoughts about something that comforts me when the hectic pace of my life frustrates my efforts to spend more time reading and studying God's Word.

Acts 4:13 [NASB] says, "Now as they observed the confidence of Peter and John, and understood that they were uneducated and untrained men, they were marveling and began to recognize them as having been with Jesus." Peter and John were useful in their ministry because they were intimately acquainted with Jesus, hearing what He taught and practicing what they had seen Him do.

We have that same opportunity for intimacy with Jesus and also the privilege of being filled with His Spirit and power. There is a knowledge of God that only the Holy Spirit can impart to me, no matter how many books, tapes or lectures I have available.

Matthew 6:17 [NASB] "Blessed are you, Simon Barjona because flesh and blood did not reveal this to you, but My Father who is in heaven."

Also, Galatians 1:15-16 [NKJV] Paul says, "But when He... was pleased to reveal His Son in me...I did not immediately consult with flesh and blood..."

In Ephesians, Paul prays for the church that God would give them a spirit of wisdom and revelation in the knowledge of Jesus. As Christians, we strive for a greater intimacy with Christ, by reading His word, spending time in prayer and meditation, and by listening as the Spirit teaches us through these efforts. I am also seeking that revelation knowledge of God that does not depend on human intelligence or education, but solely on God disclosing Himself to me in the quietness of my spirit.

Love in Him,
Chris

July, 1992

Dear Sisters in Christ,

A friend of many years, Bobbie, would frequently recount her Sunday morning church experiences, especially related to one person with whom she seemed to be in competition with.

My friend loved to sing in church and had been asked to sing solos in her church choir, and the same for her "competitor" in the congregation. On one particular Monday, the day after church, she began talking about her solo. She wasn't pleased with her performance. She told me how much better the other woman sang. There was sadness and frustration in her voice. I could tell her heart was hurting.

She relayed to me that she knew some of her notes were flat and her voice felt weak. Before I knew it, the voice of the Holy Spirit bypassed my mind and God's heart spoke to my friend out of my mouth. He asked her through me how she felt when her beloved grandchildren sang to her? Did she care if they were singing off key, or if all the words were correct, or even if they forgot the words? She got the point.

Our Father wants us to be devoted to loving him. My friend's songs were received with joy into God's ears and heart because they were from His child's loving heart, no matter any imperfections of the delivery.

I have a small plaque hanging in my kitchen with these words written on it: "In prayer, it is better to have a heart without words than words without heart." Really, our

Father's greatest delight (like any parent or grandparent) is to be loved from our hearts, no matter the imperfections of the delivery.

My friend's countenance completely changed after our short encounter.

Thank you, Abba.

Love in Christ,
Chris

January 2000

Dear Sisters in Christ,

In Deuteronomy 6:12 [NKJV] we catch a tiny glimpse of the heart of God when he warns His people Israel that when they become prosperous in the physical affairs of life, not to forget Him. That is our tendency. When life isn't pressing in on us too hard, we sometimes forget "that without Him we can do nothing" John 15 [NKJV]. Pressure, trouble, and trials remind me that I am but dust. Trouble keeps me on the cutting edge of faith; it keeps me in the shadow of His wings; it keeps me in the secret place of His tent where I can shout for joy; it keeps me in His strong tower; and it reminds me that I am really hidden in Christ in God. Trouble gives the Holy Spirit a chance to whisper to my heart that God always leads me in triumph in Christ Jesus…I am so thankful for his matchless, unbroken companionship and protection!

Love in Christ,
Chris

June, 2020

Dear Sisters in Christ,

It was one of those mornings when you feel the whole mountainous weight of all the previous sins you've ever committed fall down on your head, pass all the way through your body, and land at your feet – again! And it's all just there mocking and tormenting your mind, taking your breath away, bringing tears to your eyes! "How could I have, again?" I can hardly breathe, like being engulfed in an avalanche of sorrow, grief and repetitive, "I'm sorry!"

So, I was alone on that particular day (never the only day). Even though I had already confessed my sins and repented, I continued to beg God to "create in me a clean heart, oh God, (as waves of remembrance washed over me), and renew a right spirit within me." Psalm 51:10. [KJV]

I reminded myself "that if we confess our sins, He is faithful and just to forgive our sins and cleanse us from all unrighteousness." John 1:9 [KJV]

So, I would confess all, and then remember again. I kept telling myself that, "so far as the east is from the west has He removed our transgressions from us." Psalm 103:12 [AMP]

Just couldn't shake it that day as I drove through the city. Finally, when I turned the corner at the end of the city, I heard the quiet gentle voice of my Father speak to my spirit and mind. He simply said "Please stop it. I don't even know what you're talking about." God's word is true. He means what He says, "...as far as the east is from the west," an infinite distance, never to be remembered by Him forevermore.

My heart returned to its peace and assurance. I can truly say I still feel that remorse at times, but hearing God say to you, "Stop it," makes quick work of not dwelling on past sin.

Of course, because we have wandering hearts, we won't live sin free lives in our future, but Romans 8:1[ASV] tells me that, "There is therefore now no condemnation for those who are in Christ Jesus."

When Jesus walked to the cross that day at Calvary, He felt the weight of carrying all of mankind's sins. He saw all the sins (past, present and future) that every man and woman would commit, and He still went to the cross to forgive every single one of them. If He could not have forgiven <u>any one of them,</u> he would not have gone to the cross. He knew we would need a Savior. All sin is already forgiven because of His death and resurrection. Man's responsibility is to accept the free gift of forgiveness and salvation. When we do sin, He gives us His grace to confess our sins, and cleanses us from all unrighteousness. He freed us from the law of sin and death by becoming sin for us, and defeating death, which is the wages of sin. Thank you, our Loving Savior.

Love in Christ,
Chris

July, 2012

Dear Sisters in Christ,

It was the hottest summer anyone could remember, but my two cats didn't care. They wanted out early, as soon as my feet touched the floor. Perhaps they realized it was probably better before the sun came around the back of the house. So, since we sit outside and watch the cats while they are enjoying the outside world, I came out and sat on the patio glider with my coffee, still trying to feel awake.

While we all three sat there, I noticed that KC's (stands for Kitty Cat) ears perked up and he was obviously hearing or sensing something which frightened him. He first looked behind him, and then turned and looked straight at me. After a minute or so, he seemed more confident and unafraid as though he were reminding himself, "Oh, I'm okay. Mommy's here."

As I was processing this, I heard the whisper of the Holy Spirit within reminding me that "I'm okay. Daddy's here." He, ...will never leave me or forsake me, even until the end of the age." Matthew 28:20 [NKJV]. I'll always be okay. Our Daddy is God! Just as much as I would have saved my cat from any harm, within my power, our Heavenly Father in Psalm 32:7 [NIV] says that, "You will protect me from trouble and surround me with songs of deliverance."

Since that day I've repeated that phrase to myself many times. Perhaps that was what David was thinking when he wrote, "Though a thousand fall at your side, and ten thousand at your right hand, but it shall not approach you." Psalm 91:7

[NASB]. He knew without a doubt that his Father was there. He was okay.

While we may not be facing 11,000 soldiers ready to attack, we do suffer the attacks of the world, flesh and the devil in many forms: worries and trouble about money, health, family problems, woes of the world, and so on. But Paul says in Romans 8:31[NIV] "If God is for us, who can be against us?" In other words, "I'm okay, Daddy's here."

Love in Christ,
Chris

July, 1986

Dear Sisters in Christ,

As I was sitting on the beach a few weeks ago, I watched as a toddler and her mother were acting out what seemed to be a traditional beach ritual: baby runs from the blanket, mother calls her to come back. This continues on for a while until mother gets up from her blanket, and in the nick of time catches up with baby and firmly directs her back to the blanket where she belongs. Baby was significantly OVERRULED for her own well being.

At that second I was reminded that in all graciousness, our Heavenly Father overrules our own stubborn willfulness. I am so grateful that He is committed to, and has determined that we are to be conformed to the image of His Son (Romans 8:29) [NIV]. As we go off confidently in our own self-sufficiency and self-will, lovingly our Father continues to gently and diligently lead us back to His straight paths. It is at times like this, that we realize He is holding onto us, watching closely our every step.

Father, help us in all our ways to desire Your will and not our own, and to gratefully accept Your loving Sovereignty over us, knowing that our wellbeing is the desire of Your heart, Deuteronomy 5:29 [NIV] in Jesus' name. Amen.

Love in Jesus,
Chris

October, 2008

Dear Sisters in Christ,

During my working days, someone asked me, "What color is your world?" Emphasis on "your." I worked at a state institution for mental health, developmentally disabled and autistic individuals. It was not the cheeriest atmosphere; many workers saw no hope or gratitude about being there.

I can only guess that the questioner saw something "different" about me. I've always prayed it was God's light and joy through me that was visible – although I myself was not aware of it. Joy is one of the fruits of the Holy Spirit. His gift of joy colors my world in this way:

It's the color of God's mercy, love and kindness, as He daily loads us with undeserved benefits. It's the visible gifts in His world of nature. It's pure white like fresh fallen snow. It's the colors of every spring flower and tree, and the vivid green of grass before the heat of summer turns it brown. It's the color of the song of a bright yellow songbird, full of joy and freely given.

It's the deep pink and purple of a summer's sunset and a summer's night orange moon.

It's the indescribable splendor of Autumn trees and the stark dark figures of bare trees against a December sunset.

My world is the color of forgiveness: Red like big drops of blood on a black heart.

It's the color of truth, pure white light.
It's the color of being saved and loved.
It's the color of Heaven on earth.

Love in Christ,
Chris

PART II

SPIRITUALLY DISCERNED
REVELATIONS, SPOKEN
THROUGH THE BIBLE
OR REVEALED TO
INDIVIDUALS WALKING
WITH CHRIST

May, 2021

Dear Sisters in Christ,

Jonah 1,2 (AMP) NINEVAH

Jonah's agenda was not God's agenda. Jonah was an unwilling prophet. He thought those in Nineveh deserved the punishment God was about to pour out on them and did not want to warn them to repent. He was embittered against God and the Ninevites. He knew if they repented, God would forgive them, and relent of His plan of judgment. He knew if they repented, God would forgive them and not carry out the harm intended for them. Jeremiah 18:7 [AMP], Jonah 3:10 [AMP].

So, he ended up in the belly of a fish when he tried to thwart God's mercy. Jonah knew God, knew that God wants to bless, desires to forgive and show favor to the lost. 2 Peter 3- 9 [AMP] tells us that He "doesn't wish any to perish," meaning be lost to hell. Everyday our loving Father invites us, commands us to go to Nineveh. Matthew 28:19

"Go therefore and make disciples of all nations…". [AMP]

After we were born again and had received Jesus' righteousness as a gift, we were ready at that moment to leave this world for heaven. God chooses most times to leave us here and gives us the privilege of going to Nineveh (the whole world of the lost = Nineveh). "But how can they hear? How beautiful are the feet of those who carry the gospel of peace." Romans 10:15 [KJV]

I realize that I am Jonah! I may not get on a boat to flee or get swallowed by a fish and finally, reluctantly do as I'm told, but I am Jonah. It's not the big statement of literally running away. It is the escape to the TV, mall, movies, telephone, books, and the endless forms of excuses, busyness, burying the dead Matthew 8:21- 22 [KJV], and lo and behold, it's bedtime!

As I lay in the quiet, I hear the still small voice saying to me, "Go next door to your neighbor, go to Nineveh."

By the way, Jonah learned the hard way by God allowing him to suffer a little, that God's mercy and love are not deserved, but are given as a gift to all men.

Oh God, take my unwilling heart, my laziness, my lukewarmness, my weak concern, love and compassion for the lost, and my self-love and self-involvement. Make my heart as yours is, longing for none to perish. Make me aware and mindful of the eternal consequences if I don't go to Nineveh!

With love in Christ,
Chris

December, 2007

Dear Sisters in Christ,

Isaiah 7:14 [NASB] "Therefore, the Lord Himself will give you a sign: Behold a virgin will be with child and bear a son, and she will call his name Immanuel."

Immanuel – <u>GOD WITH US.</u> That is what the beautiful name of Jesus means: the Living, Mighty God alive in us! What wonderful, glorious, unbelievably good news! Have you heard anything better? It's the very heart of the Gospel. God, through the birth, death and resurrection of His only son, Jesus, has made the union of God and man possible. The veil was torn! God, through Christ, in us, with us, through us, for us!

What can be impossible for a man of faith if <u>God</u> is with us. What can triumph over us if <u>God</u> is with us. How can we not succeed when <u>God</u> Himself is our helper.

Has God's living Word been born in your heart? Thank Him now for dying in your place, rejoice that Jesus is "Immanuel," promising never to leave us or forsake us.

Wishing you a Blessed Christmas,
Chris

September, 1986

Dear Sisters in Christ,

2 Samuel 6:15, 16 [NIV] "...and David was dancing before the Lord with all his might...so David and all the house of Israel were bringing up the Ark of the Lord with shouting and the sound of the trumpet...Michal (David's wife) looked out of the window and saw King David leaping and dancing before the Lord, and she despised him in her heart." The wisdom of God was dancing, leaping and shouting in celebration and pure enjoyment before the Lord (v 21), however not all approved. David attributes his ability to be led of the Spirit in this way, to humility – not esteeming his own "dignity" more highly than what the Spirit would lead him to do in praise of God.

Sisters, it is not only the world that despises and rejects the wisdom of God, which looks like foolishness to man. In 1 Corinthians 3:1[NASB] Paul says, "....and I, brethren, could not speak to you as to spiritual men, but as to men of flesh, as to babes in Christ." We can't continue to desire the approval of the world. Jesus said believing in Him would ultimately separate us from even those closest to us, as it did with David and Michal. The division Christ spoke about is prevalent in families and even our churches. On a fleshly level, this can be painful, because we don't want to be different and considered unacceptable, but even if we gain the whole world of acceptance, what does it profit us if we've denied our Lord?

Instead, let us be encouraged to press on into the fullness of the Holy Spirit and expect to look foolish to the world as

David wholly embraced. By trying to remain acceptable in the sight of the world, we forfeit the deep things of God, which are spiritually discerned and not able to be received by the flesh.

With love in the Lord,
Chris

"Thoughts in Solitude"
Thomas Merton

"Lord, my hope is in what the eye has never seen. Therefore, let me not trust in visible rewards. My hope is in what the heart of man cannot feel. Therefore, let me not trust in the feelings of my heart. My hope is in what the hand of man has never touched. Do not let me trust what I can grasp between my fingers. Death will loosen my grasp and my vain hope will be gone.

Let me trust in Your mercy, not in myself. Let my hope be in Your love, not in health, strength, ability or human resources. If I trust You everything else will become for me strength, help and support. If I do not trust You, everything else will be my destruction."

January, 1987

Dear Sisters in Christ,

A headline in the local newspaper caught my eye. It said, "I have no more tears." Have you ever been there? I have. Sometimes our circumstances cause us so much hurt, heartache and grief that the natural physical and emotional response is to cry out from the depths of our being, sometimes with tears, sometimes without. This response is common to man. God's Word says that Jesus wept. Jeremiah 9:1[NASB] tells us that he prayed, "Oh, that my head were water, and my eyes a fountain of tears, that I may weep day and night." In Samuel 30:4-6 [NLT] David and his men, "Wept until they could weep no more," upon finding that their families and possessions had been taken by the Amalekites, indicating a depth of sorrow far beyond the boundaries of physical response. In fact, David's men were so distraught, they considered stoning him!

BUT, praise God, it was then that David applied some precious principles of victory! Verse 6 ends this way, "But David strengthened himself in the Lord, his God." David, "... took courage," (he encouraged himself) in the Lord. This is something Jesus commanded us to do in Mark 6:50 [NLT] when He told the Apostles, "Don't be afraid...Take courage! I am here!" In Mark 5:36 [KJV] Jesus told Jairus, "Don't be afraid, only believe." What are we to believe? Jesus said while praying to the Father, "Thy word is Truth," [John 17:17) [KJV] What God says is the truth about any situation. Proverbs 3:5, 6 [NLT] tells us to, "Trust in the Lord with all your heart, and do not *depend on your own understanding.* Seek His will in all you do and He will show you which path to take." The Psalmist said in Psalm 42:5 [NLT] "Why am I discouraged? Why is my heart so sad? I will put my hope in God! I will praise Him again, my Savior and my God." He remembered what God had done in the past.

So, getting back, David (and really ourselves as well) may not have "felt" like doing it in the flesh, but by faith he made a conscious effort in the midst of tragedy to remind himself of God's Words, God's opinions on the matter, and God's truth which is forever settled in heaven. Praise His Name! David's mind was trained to remember God, El Shaddai, the all sufficient One. It is our privilege as well to encourage ourselves in the Lord, seek His direction, and expect that He will be a present help in trouble. Psalm 32:7 [NLT] says that, "You surround me with songs of victory." In everything, "... those who wait upon the Lord shall renew their strength." Isaiah 40:31 [NJKV]

God bless you,
Chris

This Thanksgiving, I'd like to share a
few lines from a favorite poem:

THANKSGIVING

Thank You, Father, for Your magnificence in nature.
Thank You, Father, for the inner promptings of Your Spirit.
Thank You, Father, for fresh truth to live by.
Thank You, Father, for those who inspire me, love me.
Lord, help us to think first of those things which will benefit others
Before we begin listing our own needs.
Give us grace to live in such a way that we draw attention to You. Amen

Brian Jeffrey Leech

December, 1987

Dear Sisters in Christ,

My heart's desire this Christmas is to live daily the reality of the incarnation of Jesus Christ. Philippians 2:5-8 [NASB] says, "Have this attitude in yourselves which was also in Christ Jesus, who although He existed in the form of God, did not regard equality with God a thing to be grasped, but emptied Himself, taking the form of a bond servant, and being made in the likeness of man. And being found in appearance as a man, He humbled Himself by becoming obedient to the point of death, even death on a cross." Jesus willingly left His glorious heavenly home to come to earth as a servant and a sacrifice. He let go of everything heavenly, and laid claim to nothing earthly that He might reclaim a fallen human race. Jesus tells us that if we desire to follow Him, we also must deny ourselves, take up our cross daily, and let go of our "right" to anything, save the command of the Lord. Jesus said He came to do the Father's will, that this was His "bread," his sustenance, that which satisfied His spiritual hunger. He sends us to do the same. Living in and doing the Father's will is the joy, satisfaction and reality of living the incarnation – the only bread that truly satisfies the human spirit. I wish you all a joyous celebration of the birth of our precious Savior, Jesus.

Love in Him,
Chris

I STAND BY THE DOOR

A few lines of another favorite and meaningful poem:

I stand by the door. I neither go too far in, nor stay too far out.
It is the door through which men walk when they find God.
There's no use my going way inside and staying there,
When so many are still outside, craving to know where the door is.
They creep along the wall with outstretched, groping hands; feeling
For a door, knowing there must be a door, yet they never find it...

...So, I Stand By The Door

Samuel Shoemaker
From: "The Life of Samuel Shoemaker"

INTIMATE WALK

By Chris Trainor

And Jesus, you capture me
And all my hidden silence.
You whisper to me in
Unspeakable poetry
And in music beyond melody
You embrace and enclose me
Within you.
We are no longer separate.
Yet You are too near to comprehend
Your every breath and slightest
Movement and casual glance
Proceed from a source so much
Deeper than I could ever touch in
Understanding.

Why do you speak to me so poor
In perception? So weak in
Acceptance.
I do not know how to listen to
Your gentle words of love:
These words which have the power
To transform me into something
Beautiful and incomprehensible
As Yourself.
Your fingers touch my face
Always so softly, softly.
Despite my wonder, You continue to
Draw me onward to
Fertile and unimaginable places,
Never known before except in

Unconscious dreams.
And always your beauty pains me.
Not knowing whether to shout in joy,
Or ache silently, I am compelled to reach
Out for your kiss.
Jesus, I trust your Love.

PART III

JESUS' FINAL INSTRUCTIONS TO HIS MOST INTIMATE FAITHFUL FOLLOWERS; THOSE WHO LOVED, LISTENED TO, AND OBEYED HIM

June 2021

Dear Sisters in Christ,

His Last Words,

I wanted to share this devotion with you, because there's something about "last words" in general that make them very important, something that needs to be said, some unsaid confession, some advice the speaker just couldn't say until the last minute.

Jesus didn't wait until the end. He spoke these words in many forms throughout His ministry. But Matthew's gospel ascribes them as Jesus' last directions and commands to His precious Apostles in Matthew 28:18-20 [KJV] before His ascension in Bethany.

"All authority in heaven and on earth has been given to me. Go therefore and teach all nations, baptizing them in the name of the Father, and of the Son, and of the Holy Spirit. Teaching them to observe all things whatsoever I have commanded you. I am with you always, even to the end of the age."

From Luke's gospel 24:46-48 in the Common English Bible translation, this is what is written, "The Christ will suffer, die and rise from the dead on the third day, and a change of heart and life for the forgiveness of sins must be preached in His name to all nations beginning from Jerusalem. You are witnesses of these things."

Two verses that I feel are important companions to these last words of Christ are:

1. Zechariah 4:6 [KJV] this is the Lord's Word to Zerubbabel, "Not by might, nor by power, but by my Spirit says the Lord of Hosts."
2. "And the gospel is the power of God unto Salvation to everyone that believes." Romans 1:16 [ASV].

In other words, all of the followers of Christ are called to action in His command to "Go." We must understand though that it is God who does the work of changing hearts and turning them to Himself. In I Kings 18:37 [AMP], Elijah was seeking a great outpouring of God's power and His prayer was, "Answer me, oh Lord, answer me that this people know that you, oh Lord, have turned their hearts back to God."

The reason God can freely and righteously turn the hearts of sinners is because that is what Jesus bought for all men by His death and Resurrection.

In Jeremiah 31:33 [AMP], God, speaking of the future after Christs' sacrifice says, "I will put my law within them, and I will write it on their hearts and I will be their God,

And they will be my people".

As Christians, Scripture tells us that "the power in us is greater than the power in the world." (The Holy Spirit V. Satan) But if we're not connected to and accessing that power, then, as Jesus says, "The flesh profits nothing," John 6:63 [NKJV], "What shall we present to our Heavenly Father in light of His great goodness and grace – gold, silver, jewels, wood, hay, or straw?" I Corinthians 3:12-13 [CEB].

Although it is God who does the work, He is commanding in Matthew 28:19, [CEB] asking us to be willing to go, whether next door, down the street, across the country or across the world. All of our appointed mission fields won't be the same. Think of the Apostle Philip who was sent by the Holy Spirit to go to a specific place (Gaza) to do a specific task, speak to the Ethiopian Eunuch. Will we be a Philip or a Jonah?

Our obedience and faithfulness to what He asks of us involves the "laying down of our lives, our own agendas, desires for self-gratification, for the pleasures of this world, even for the need to give our own opinions or the need to speak at all. In a world ruled by social media, the option to always be "outside" of ourselves, speaking our minds, deprives us of time in the secret place of quiet meditation with our Lord, where the Holy Spirit relays His instruction for our actions. Philip heard the voice of the Spirit and was available to go. In Romans 12:1 [NASB], Paul tells us "to present our bodies as living sacrifices as our reasonable service of worship."

When God does open doors and gives us His plan to go, we must be prepared to speak. The Spirit will bring to mind what we are to say about Jesus and salvation, but if we don't study to show ourselves approved, we shall be at a loss for the word to hear or to say. How can we share what we don't know? We must be prepared with knowledge of Jesus' teachings and words and actions.

In Philippians 1:9 [CEB] Paul writes, "This is my prayer, that you might become more and more rich with knowledge and all kinds of insight." God's plan for the redemption of His fallen creatures and creation itself was by Him persistently and protectively threaded, from the timeless dimension of eternity past. The Lamb of God, Jesus, was slain before the foundation of the world for the redemption of the world. (Revelation 13:8) [KJV]. God drew the scarlet thread of Christ's redeeming blood throughout the ages. He knew we would need a Savior. Ephesians 1:4 [CEB] tells us that "God also chose us (believers and followers of Christ) in Christ to be holy and blameless in God's presence before the foundation of the world," and chose us to partake in God's plan of redemption. As Christians assume the responsibility of sharing the truth of the Gospel, in Romans 10:14 [NLT], Paul asks these questions, "And how can they believe in Him if they have never heard about Him" and 10:15, [NLT] "That is why the Scriptures say, "How beautiful are the feet of the messengers who bring good news!"

We are a body of believers. Each part of a body has a different function in obeying Jesus' last words, "Some will sow, some will reap," John 4:37-38 [KJV].

Lastly, we must be living examples of hearts changed by Christ. 2 Corinthians 5:20-21[KJV] (Paul speaking), "Now then, we are ambassadors for Christ, as God did beseech you by us: we pray you in Christ's stead, be ye reconciled to God. For He has made Him (Jesus) to be sin for us, who knew no sin, that we might be made the Righteousness of God in Him."

We must pursue righteousness in all our decisions, fight the good fight against "the world, the flesh and the devil."

In 1 Corinthians 9:27 [KJV] Paul says that he, "Keeps his body under and brings it into subjection, lest by any means, when I have preached to others, I myself should be cast away."

God bless you Sisters in Christ
as you pursue obedience to Christ's great Commission to
spread his glorious gospel. Love in Christ, Chris

Printed in the United States
by Baker & Taylor Publisher Services